If you were me and lived in...
BRAZIL

A Child's Introduction to Culture Around the World

Carole P. Roman

Illustrated by Kelsea Wierenga

For Lady Selah Sujuris and the team at the Storyteller's Campfire Blogtalk Radio. Thank you for your unwavering support.

If you were me and lived in Brazil (Bra-zil), your home would be known as the Federative Republic of Brazil, which is the largest country in South America.

It is the largest Portuguese-speaking (Por-tu-geeze) country in the world. The people speak Portuguese there because the explorer, Pedro Álvares Cabral (Ped-ro Al-ver-es Ca-br-al), declared it as a part of Portugal in the 1500s.

Brazil produces the most coffee in the world.

You might live in the capital, Brasília (Bra-sil-ya). In 1960, they moved the capital from Rio de Janeiro (Ree-o de Jan-nea-rou) to the more centrally located Brasilia. It is a beautiful city, and all the branches of the government are located there. The president of Brazil lives in a modern palace near the man-made Lake Paranoá (Par-a-nu-a).

If you were a boy, your parents might have chosen Lucas (Loo-cas), Paulo (Pau-lo), or Bruno (Brew-no) as your name. Gabriela (Gab-ree-el-la), Ana (An-a), and Natália (Na-ta-lia) are some of the popular names for girls.

Mamãe (Ma-mae) is what you would call your mommy. Papai (Pap-aye) is the name for your daddy.

When you go to the mercearia (mer-ser-ree-ya) with Mamãe, you would use a Brazilian real (Bra-zil-yun rey-al) to purchase leite (lay-chee), pão (pa-oo), and queijo (kay-zo). That means you would be buying milk, bread, and cheese. Can you guess where you would go and which of the words translate to milk, bread, and cheese?

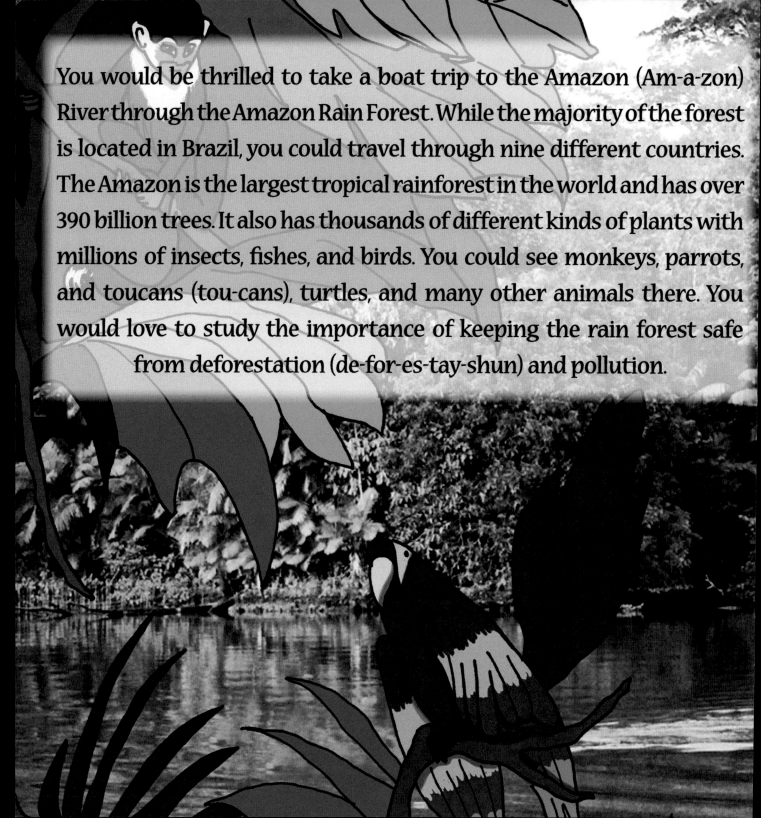

You would be thrilled to take a boat trip to the Amazon (Am-a-zon) River through the Amazon Rain Forest. While the majority of the forest is located in Brazil, you could travel through nine different countries. The Amazon is the largest tropical rainforest in the world and has over 390 billion trees. It also has thousands of different kinds of plants with millions of insects, fishes, and birds. You could see monkeys, parrots, and toucans (tou-cans), turtles, and many other animals there. You would love to study the importance of keeping the rain forest safe from deforestation (de-for-es-tay-shun) and pollution.

Mamãe would make your favorite stew called moqueca (mo-keh-kah). Shrimp and a variety of fish would be steamed in a clay pot with tomatoes, onions, and spices with rice as a side dish. Sometimes she would add peppers and coconut milk to make it special. The churrasqueira (chir-ras-co) is where Papai would barbecue (bar-bee-que) the meat outside. It is a large grill where he would cook beef, lamb, chicken hearts, and sausage. You always wait for Mamãe to leave the room so you can steal pão de queijo (pow de kay-so) from the table. It is a crispy ball of baked bread and cheese and is delicious.

Of course, you know you can't have dessert until after you finish your dinner. Brigadeiros (Brig-a-der-os) are a combination of condensed milk, butter, sugar, and cocoa powder formed into small circles of sweetness. They are tasty treats rolled in sprinkles and so very sweet.

You constantly compare futebol (fut-bol) moves with your cousin in New York. They tease you and tell you the game is really called soccer. You laugh and respond that the whole world calls it futebol!

While you would never miss a home game at the stadium, you also love swimming, tennis, volleyball, and watching motorsports.

The Brazilian Grand Prix (Bra-zil-yun Grand Pree) is a fast race with a large prize for the winner. It takes place on a special race course and is thrilling to watch.

You may prefer to play Cinco Marias (Sin-ko Ma-ree-yas) with a bunch of your friends outside. You would place five small pebbles near each other on the ground. One of you would pick up the first stone, toss it in the air, and try to pick up one of the pebbles off the ground. In the next round, you would try to pick up two and then three, until all of the stones are picked up before the first pebble hits the floor. The player that picks up all four stones is the winner.

Your sister would not play because she doesn't like to let go of her boneca (bon-ek-ca). You tell her that you need two hands to play Cinco Marias, but she never listens to you.

Do you know what a boneca is?

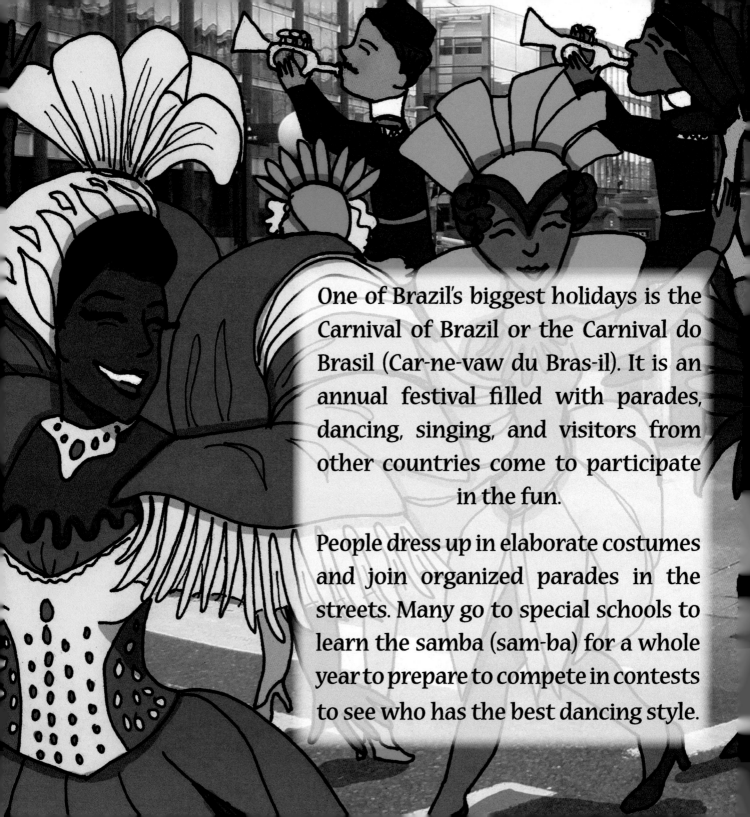

One of Brazil's biggest holidays is the Carnival of Brazil or the Carnival do Brasil (Car-ne-vaw du Bras-il). It is an annual festival filled with parades, dancing, singing, and visitors from other countries come to participate in the fun.

People dress up in elaborate costumes and join organized parades in the streets. Many go to special schools to learn the samba (sam-ba) for a whole year to prepare to compete in contests to see who has the best dancing style.

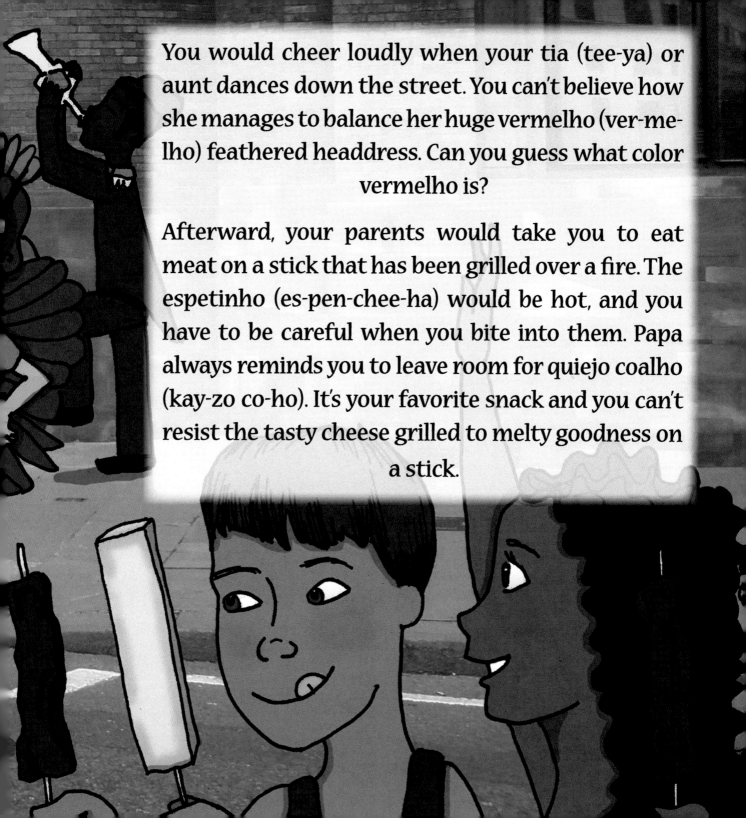

You would cheer loudly when your tia (tee-ya) or aunt dances down the street. You can't believe how she manages to balance her huge vermelho (ver-me-lho) feathered headdress. Can you guess what color vermelho is?

Afterward, your parents would take you to eat meat on a stick that has been grilled over a fire. The espetinho (es-pen-chee-ha) would be hot, and you have to be careful when you bite into them. Papa always reminds you to leave room for quiejo coalho (kay-zo co-ho). It's your favorite snack and you can't resist the tasty cheese grilled to melty goodness on a stick.

You would tell your friends about your carnival adventure when you go to escola (es-co-la). Can you guess where you would be?

So you see, if you were me, how life in Brazil could really be.

Pronunciation Guide

Amazon (Am-a-zon)- a huge rainforest teaming with a wide variety of plants, fish, and animals.

Ana (An-a)- a popular girl's name in Brazil.

barbecue (bar-bee-que)- a popular way to roast meats over an open fire.

Brazil (Bra-zil)- the Federative Republic of Brazil, which is the largest country in South America.

Brazilian real (Bra-zil-yun rey-al)- money in Brazil.

Brazilian Grand Prix (Bra-zil-yun Grand Pree)- a great sports car race.

Brasilia (Bra-sil-ya)- the capital of Brazil.

Brigadeiros (Brig-a-der-os)- tiny rolled balls that are delightful sweet treats of condensed milk, sugar, butter, and cocoa.

boneca (bon-ek-ca)- a doll.

Bruno (Brew-no)- a popular boy's name in Brazil.

Carnaval do Brasil (Car-ne-vaw Bras-il) – an annual festival filled with parades, dancing, singing, and visitors from other countries.

churrasqueira (chir-ras-co) a large grill used for barbecuing meats in Brazil.

Cinco Marias (Sin-ko Ma-ree-yas)- a popular children's game in Brazil similar to jacks.

deforestation (de-for-es-tay-shun)- the cutting down the valuable trees in the rain forest.

escola (es-co-la)- a school.

espetinho (es-pen-chee-ha)- a sausage or chicken grilled on a stick.

futebol (fut-bol)- soccer

Gabriela (Gab-ree-el-la)- a popular girl's name in Brazil.

Lake Paranoa (Par-a-nu-a)- the artificially created lake in the capital of Brazil.

leite (lay-chee)- milk.

Lucas (Loo-cas)- a popular boy's name in Brazil.

Mamãe (Ma-mae)- Mommy.

mercearia (mer-ser-ree-ya)- the market.

moqueca (mo-keh-kah)- a fish stew made with shrimp and fish. Served with rice on the side.

Natalia (Na-ta-lia)- a popular girl's name in Brazil.

pao (pa-oo)- bread.

pao de queijo (pa-oo de kay-zo)- tasty round baked dumplings of bread and cheese.

Papai (Pap-aye)- Daddy.

Paulo (Pau-lo)- a popular boy's name in Brazil.

Pedro Alvares Cabral (Ped-ro Al-ver-es Ca-br-al)- an explorer who claimed Brazil in the 1500s.

Portuguese (Por-tu-geeze)- the language spoken in both Brazil and Portugal.

queijo (kay-zo)- cheese.

quiejo coalho (kay-so col-ho)- grilled cheese on a stick.

Rio de Janeiro (Ree-o de Jan-nea-rou)- the second largest city in Brazil and the original capital of the country. Its name means River of January because it was discovered and named by the Portuguese explorers in January.

samba (sam-ba)- a Brazilian dance of African origin.

sloths (sl-oths)- a medium-sized mammal that lives in the trees.

tia (tee-ya)- an aunt.

toucan (tou-cans)- a bird with a large beak.

vermelho (ver-me-lho)- the color red.

Made in the USA
Monee, IL
22 October 2021